The Bravest Bear I know

A story of bravery in the face of the enemy

by

Michael Parkin

2014

This little book is dedicated to all men, women, horses, dogs, pigeons and, yes, even teddy bears of whatever shape or size, who served in the Great War 1914-1918.

Their memory will last for ever.

Contents

The Bravest Bear I know

1. The Story through Time

Great, Great Grandad Albert Clarkson	1897 - 1955
Albert was nine when he received Jo Bear	1906
Albert left school and went down the pit	1911
The Great War began in August	1914
Albert joined the Army and went to war	1915
Albert invalided back home in spring	1918
The Great War ended 11th November	1918
Jo Bear came home to Albert	1920
Great Grandad Michael	1924 - 1986
Albert gave Jo to his son, Michael	1933
Grandad George was born	1950
Michael gave Jo to his son George	1959
Peter's father David was born	1973
David, received Jo as a present	1982
Peter Clarkson was born	2005
Peter was nine and was given Jo Bear	2014

2. The Great War

All good stories have a little magic, a pinch of luck, a smattering of disaster woven into an engaging tale. I hope this tale has all these. Amongst the mud, dust, blood, fear and excitement of a war there is usually some goodness and some bravery to report. Whilst we should look forward to the future we must never forget the lessons of the past and the people who gave their all for us. Yes, even a teddy bear!

The **'Great War'** or, as H.G. Wells named it 'the war to end all wars', began on 28th July 1914 and ended, precisely, at 11 am Wednesday 11th November 1918. Many different countries contributed men and all suffered terrible casualties. I know the numbers are hard to imagine but Britain and her allies lost around 1 million men killed and over 1.5 million injured. One million is roughly equivalent to the whole population of Derbyshire and Nottinghamshire, including the cities, to-day!

The main armies were from Germany and Great Britain. Space does not allow me to mention all those who took part; but I recognise, in particular, members of the British Commonwealth, France and, towards the end of the War, the United States of America.

It was definitely not the 'war to end all wars' as suggested in the 1920's nor, in my opinion, was it a 'Great' war unless we count it was the most devastating. We now use the term 'First World War' which, implying it was not the last, is all you really need to know. Even to-day, we are still fighting wars and killing people in various parts of the World. It is clear that the millions of casualties of the 'Great War' had and continue to have little impact on the decisions of the men who lead us to-day – and I use the word 'men' intentionally.

All of the people who fought in this terrible war and survived are no longer with us; they have joined their comrades who did not live to see the end of it. However, we are not short of information about the war. There are official and unofficial records, films, photographs, memories, diaries, poems, artistic impressions and miles of print to remind us of the causes, the details and the outcomes. Of course, not all of this can be relied on as absolute truth, if the truth really exists.

The centenary, one hundred years, from the start of the war will see a great many reprinted books and even some new ones. This story is very different, it does not seek to explain why the war started or even the tactics involved. It is not about fighting and killing, it is about bravery and loyalty. It is one young man's experiences and of how the war changed his life. It is really the story of a teddy bear, a very small stuffed toy.

It must be difficult for most people to understand the emotions felt by people in the period around the beginning of this war and continuing until 1918. It is reported that in 1918 United States Senator Hiram Warren Johnson said, "The first casualty when war comes is truth". Since then others have claimed this statement but it matters not; this particular story has a logical ring of 'truth' about it.

There is no political or nationalistic edge to the story; it is one young man's record – he was, in actual fact, English but he could easily have been German, Russian or even Turkish. It is for you to decide whether it is true or not. I like to think that it is. Why would Albert write it down if it were not true?

We will start with a boy's ninth birthday party in 2014 and let us see where we go from this.

3. A Special Present

"Thanks mum that was a great party, the best ever."

Peter Clarkson's birthday party had been really 'cool'. He had watched his mum working all day at the food, cleaning the house and wrapping 'pass-the-parcel' bundles. She was even picking out suitable music for the party and setting out the big dining table with cakes, sandwiches, crisps and a mixture of goodies. What Peter didn't know then was that his birthday was to lead to an even more exciting story and an experience very different from any other birthday.

It was the 11th November and Peter was now nine years old. He was feeling really grown-up as he stood at the front door with his mum watching all his friends on their way home. Some were walking to their homes close by and others had been collected by their parents in cars. It had been a fantastic party with loads of games, some great laughs and everybody seemed to have enjoyed it. He had been given loads of presents - they were all piled up on the sideboard – books, 'T' shirts, an England rugby jersey, DVDs and even boxes of sweets. His mum and dad had given him a laptop and that was what he wanted most of all, he wouldn't have to use dad's computer now; he felt really lucky.

On top of all that, Simon Spencer, his best friend from next door, had been sick on the kitchen floor after eating too much pork pie and trifle (I don't think mum should have put sherry in it!); that was really gross! Nigel Spencer had one of his nose-bleeds and mum had to use two tea towels to soak up the blood. Elizabeth Jones, from the big house at the end of the street, had been showing off and dropped her new iPod into the fish tank. Everybody thought that was great fun, except perhaps the goldfish! Imagine going round and round all day listening to Elizabeth's favourite boy band, One Direction.

Well, that was all OK but it is not really the story I want to tell you, let me continue.

When his friends had left, Peter sat with his mum eating a plate of sandwiches; he had been too excited to eat anything at the party. It had been a tiring but exciting day.

Dad had been missing upstairs for a while and when he came down he was holding a battered old cardboard box tied up with thick brown string; the sort of box that you get when you buy new shoes but this box wasn't new, in fact it was falling apart.

"Peter, I want to give you something extra, a special present, something you must look after very, very carefully. My father gave it to me when I was nine a few years ago and I have been keeping it for you all this time."

He opened the box and held up a brown teddy bear, not a new bear but an old, scruffy teddy bear with some clumps of fur missing cuts and a miserable look on its face. The bear was about half a metre high with cuts on his ears and dirty stains on his legs and arms. The bear looked a real mess.

"Is this a joke?" exclaimed Peter. *"Where did you get it from? It's rubbish!"*

"No, it's not a joke, his name is Joseph, or just Jo," explained his father, *"and he used to belong to my father, his father and his father before him. He was given to your great, great grandfather when he was nine, just like you are to-day, but in 1906. Would you believe that this scruffy little teddy bear is more than 100 years old, in fact at least 108?"*

Peter looked at the bear in absolute amazement; he didn't know what to make of it. He had never seen a teddy bear quite so tatty and worn. It certainly didn't look like anyone loved it. But there was one special thing about the bear that shone bright and clear and that was his piercing blue eyes. In fact, wherever you looked the eyes seemed to follow you around the room. "*Weird,*" thought Peter.

"*You must promise me that you will look after Joseph, keep him safe and then if you ever have a child of your own you must give the bear to him. Of course, you won't be able to play with him or let any of your friends play with him, but you can keep him in your bedroom.*"

"*Dad, I'm nine and I'm a boy, I don't play with teddy bears! And, there's no way I'm going to tell any of my friends that I've had a **teddy bear** for my ninth birthday.*"

Peter's father passed the bear over to him and as he held it he could feel that it was actually very thin, some stuffing was missing from the arms and legs; it also smelt dusty and dirty, like damp soil or, Peter thought to himself, the bottom of his rabbit's hutch. Despite this Peter had a strange feeling that the bear was looking straight into his eyes; but that might have been his imagination.

As Peter sat looking at the bear and wondering what to do with it, he was attracted to a small furry pocket sawn onto his tummy. It was a bit like the ones that kangaroos have to keep their babies in, you know a pouch, but smaller. Peter managed to squeeze two fingers into the pocket and he found a small piece of paper at the very bottom amongst the dust. As he pulled the paper he could see it was yellow and tatty fell into several pieces on the table.

"Let me see Peter, this is fascinating, I never noticed that pocket when I got the bear. This little paper note must be donkey's year's old," said dad, *"I wonder who put it there."* In truth both of them were getting quite excited. Peter and his dad set about piecing the bits of paper together.

The paper was in several different shaped fragments that didn't quite fit together – like those puzzles you get in a Christmas cracker. They could see some words and numbers written on them but neither Peter nor his dad could read all of the words or even understand them. They set the pieces out in a square and could see the words 'artillery', '4,000', 'reserve', 'advance' and more numbers. They could not make out a sentence as the rest of writing was smudged and the paper pieces were faded and stained with dirt and the effects of age.

Whilst dad was trying to make sense of the paper note, Peter began to examine the old bear a little more closely, he noticed a tiny cardboard disc pinned to chest with a tiny rusty safety pin. *"What's this label dad?"*

By this time Peter's dad had found the magnifying glass, the big round one that his mother used for her embroidery and he tried to read the words. *"You can't read it clearly but if you look closely you can to see that it says **'Jo, The Bravest Bear I know'**."*

"Wow, what does that all mean?" asked Peter.

"I can't remember the whole story, no-one has talked about it for years, but your grandfather George might remember some of it. It was something about your great, great grandfather taking the bear with him when he went to the Great War. I don't suppose it's true but I'll ask him if you want. In fact we could go to see him on Saturday morning. I wonder if he knows about the paper in the bear's pocket, he never told me about that either."

"Do you think he's too young to understand all this about war?" remarked Peter's mother, who was looking on with interest, *"It's so long ago and we're supposed to be having*

fun on his birthday. Shouldn't you wait until he's a little older?"

"**Mu-um**, I am nine I can understand everything," protested Peter in as grown up manner as he could. Maybe he did understand and maybe he didn't, we shall see. However, Peter was clearly intrigued by the bear and his story.

"I don't know, it's a sort of family tradition. The bear was given to me when I was nine and I've kept it ever since. Do you really understand, Peter?"

"I'll keep it if you want me to dad, I'll put it in my suit-case with the special things on the top of my wardrobe. Can we see if we can find out more of his story, it might be good?"

Peter's dad wrapped the bear in some tissue paper and carefully placed him back in the box and put it on the sideboard. To be honest with the all the excitement of the party and his pile of real presents, especially the laptop, Peter soon forgot all about the bear, for a couple of days at least.

On Saturday morning after breakfast dad reminded Peter that they were going to see Grandad George about the bear story.

"Wow, I forgot about the bear, shall I take him with me?" said Peter. They set off for grandad's house and I don't really know who was the most excited. The story was probably more of an interest to dad than his son at this stage but that would change. Anyway, Peter always looked forward to seeing his grandad.

"So you finally got Old Jo Bear," said Grandad as they sat around his kitchen table, *"I gave it to your dad when he was nine. You didn't really want it, did you?"* turning to Peter's dad, *"I had to save it until you left home to get married. You weren't really interested, which I thought was a shame."* Peter's dad looked a little embarrassed at this remark and didn't say anything.

"I'd like to know more about my Great Grandad and the war, we're been doing some project work on world wars at school," added Peter.

"Well, it's not your Great Grandad, Peter, it's your **Great, Great** Grandad Albert. He died when I was five so I can hardly remember him. By the way, when I got the old bear my father told me there was a story written about his adventures in a notebook. Did I give it to you?" Grandad asked Peter's dad.

"Not as I remember, dad, I don't recall anything about a book or a story."

"No, but you weren't really interested were you, too busy playing football."

"Well, **I'm** interested," added Peter eagerly, looking at his father and then at his grandfather.

"I'm not sure where to look for it, all I've got left from my dad is a box of old black and white photographs and I've not been into that box for years. I'll see if I can find it. You've got to understand Peter that people who had been fighting in the wars didn't usually talk about it. It brings back sad memories about their friends who are no longer around and they saw lots of nasty things they do not really want to think about."

Then he disappeared into the spare room and eventually came back with a big old wooden box which he set on the coffee table. Grandad pulled out piles of old photographs in packets. They all got distracted and began looking for old pictures from holidays and trips years ago, before Peter was born. Within a couple of minutes Peter's dad and his father were lost in their memories. Peter was keen to find the book but he was having no luck.

"It doesn't look as if it's there," said Grandad, *"I'm not surprised it's been a long time, it may just have dropped to pieces or been thrown away."*

Peter was still ferreting about in the big box. *"Wait a minute, what's this in the bottom of the box?"* He wrestled a few sheets of old paper from the box.

"That's only old sheets of newspaper, I used it as a lining, you can pull it out if you want."

Peter pulled out the sheets of old newspaper; it was all dusty and yellow. As he pulled at the paper it crumbled to pieces in his hand.

"I'll get yesterday's newspaper we'll put some new lining in. I must show these old photographs to your grandma when she comes back from shopping. She'll really enjoy that; it must be years since we looked at them."

Just as Peter was screwing up the old newspaper he felt something a little harder and stiffer in between the sheets. He carefully opened the folds of the old newspaper and pulled out an old notebook with a speckled cardboard cover.

"Grandad, look at this, is this it?" by this time Peter was getting really excited.

Not surprisingly, Peter's father and his Grandad David put down the old photographs they have been looking at and became very interested in Peter's find.

"Can I look," said his Grandad.

Peter passed the old exercise book to his Grandad and looked on, hardly able to control himself. This was going to be good, he thought to himself. Peter took Jo Bear out of the box he had brought him in and sat him on his knee for good luck!

"Goodness me, yes, this is it. Peter look here can your read what it says on the first page? Is that Old Jo, I haven't seen him for years, I can see he's still in one piece, just."

Peter looked at the first page of the notebook. He read out the words, ***"This is the tale of the Bravest Bear I know."***

"That's what it says on the bear's label. Will you read it Grandad, please?" asked Peter, too excited to read it himself.

Grandad looked at Peter, at the book and at his son, Peter's father.

"It will be quite sad, I imagine, but exciting at the same time. I'm not really sure it's suitable for a nine-year old. I do remember seeing the book before but I never read it. Now let me see . . ."

*"**Please**, please Grandad. I want to hear about Jo and great, great, great Grandad Albert."* They smiled at Peter getting his 'greats' all mixed up. He had added one too many this time.

Grandad dug his reading glasses out of his shirt pocket. As he opened the book to read it didn't feel quite right. He felt something heavy in the back cover. He turned the book over and opened the back page.

Grandad almost dropped the notebook. They could all see a large silver medal in the shape of a big coin, bigger than a £2 coin, with a blue ribbon with white and red bands down the middle. *"This is a very special medal look it's got my grandfather's name all around the edge. It says 'Pte A. Clarkson 109887621 Pte means that he was a Private Solider, that was his rank."*

After looking at the name on the edge, Peter turned the medal over and read the words on the back; it read '**For BRAVERY in the FIELD**'. *"What does that mean Grandad?"*

"It means it was presented for being extremely brave on the battlefield." Grandad thought for a moment, *"All the soldiers were brave, just even being there, but some did special things and were given a medal like this."*

Grandad sat quietly for a moment, *"I never knew my grandfather was awarded the Military Medal for bravery.*

Nobody ever told me. Wait a minute, what do these words on this envelope say?"

Grandad, who was now getting a little emotional, read out the last few words on the envelope stuck in the back of the book. *"I was awarded the Military Medal for bravery but I was never as brave as this bear. I want to award the medal to Joseph Bear MM."*

"Look at the back," shouted Peter, *"there are some more medals, three of them, wow, this is great."*

Grandad examined the three medals carefully, *"I know about these, they are war medals issued to all soldiers who took part in the war. The men had a silly nick-name for them it was 'Pip, Squeak and Wilfred'. I think it was something to do with a stage act at that time. If you look you can see my Grandad's name on the edge or across the back of each one. Pte A. Clarkson 109887621."*

There was a gold coloured star with a red white and blue ribbon, a round medal with a blue white and orange ribbon and a gold coloured medal with a multi-coloured ribbon, like a rainbow.

To be honest, I think the medals seemed to mean more to Peter's Grandad than his father because he seemed to lose himself in his thoughts for a few minutes.

"Anyway," he said eventually, clearing his throat, *"we had better look at the story now."*

He made himself comfortable and turned to the front of the little speckled note book.

It must have been funny to see both Peter and his father watching the old man, eagerly waiting for the story. Peter, still with the old teddy bear on his knee.

4. Albert's Story

This is the story Peter's grandfather David began to read. .

Albert's Story

I'm setting down this tale for my children, if I am ever lucky enough to have any. I am not going to write about the nasty side of this war, although most of it was horrible, really terrible. This is actually about a bear, a small, rather tatty, teddy bear. He was with me for years, through thick and thin, until I was injured then he disappeared – or so I thought.

I was nine when my father gave me a teddy bear for me birthday. They were all the rage at that time, I think they were named after the old American President 'Teddy' Roosevelt. It was around 1906 I think.

But, it was in 1920 when I was re-united with my old teddy bear, Joseph. I had been wounded towards the end of the war and sent home in spring 1918 to recuperate - what my mates called a 'Blighty wound'. The war actually ended in November 1918.

'Blighty' is what we called England or Britain, it means an injury that is serious enough to be moved from the front line and sent home, that is, of course, if you survived. I did survive but I was never able to go back to the war. I was lucky in a way, many of my friends were not so lucky.

I thought I had lost all my belongings, including Old Jo Bear. When my old army pal, Stan Fellows, was demobbed from the army he stayed in London for a while and he didn't get back home until sometime in 1920. When he found out I was living with my parents he came to see me and he brought a carrier bag with all my stuff. He told me he'd had it in his kit bag from the time I was wounded; he told me he was one of the stretcher bearers who carried me out of 'no man's land' and handed me over to the medics.

When I tipped the bag out I found a few old letters from home, a rusty penknife, spare tunic buttons, a pair of socks, even a couple of rifle bullets and my old teddy bear Jo. He did look in a sorry state but, as old as I was, I was really pleased to see him.

"Grandad, what is 'no man's land'?" asked Peter.

"Well," replied Grandad removing his spectacles, "It's the stretch of land between the two lines of soldiers in their trenches, the Germans on one side and the British and French on the other. It is the land in the middle that neither side has won or holds; a very dangerous piece of land. It might become clearer to understand when I read on." He hung his reading glasses back on his nose. Peter moved a little closer to the edge of his seat, still clutching Jo Bear on his knee.

When Stan wasn't looking I felt in Jo's little pocket and the secret note was still there at the bottom. Jo had looked after it all this time. What a brave little bear! I didn't want to tell Stan about the note.

Stan and me spent a few hours reminiscing over a few beers and talking about the fun we had – not the bad times, for some reason no-body wanted to talk about the bad times! We chatted about some of our mates who had survived and where they had got to. We reminded each other about the rats as big as cats, the fleas that nibbled at you all day, the sergeants shouting at everybody and even the cold, stewed tea. It's funny what you remember.

When Stan had left, I got to thinking I ought to write down Jo's story. It took me a few months to get round to it but I eventually did and here it is. If I have a son I will give it to him together with Jo Bear. I am not too good at writing and spelling so I might repeat myself or get things in the wrong order but here we go.

It all started in 1906 when I was nine when my mum and dad gave me a teddy bear for my birthday. It was a smart brown bear and I called him Joseph Bear, usually just 'Jo'. I remember this quite well, I didn't play with the bear much as I preferred my tin soldiers but he did live in my bedroom. As I had no brothers or sisters I used to talk to Jo when I was lonely, which was quite often. He became more of a close friend than a toy, strange really! In fact, I always thought he had strange eyes and he was looking straight at me.

I left school when I was 14 and started work with my dad who worked at the local pit as an underground deputy. My job was to help with the ponies who worked underground and carted wooden pit props and supplies to the coal face and then tubs of coal back to the pit bottom. I didn't enjoy the work, it was hard and boring (apart from the pit ponies who were my best mates underground) and I made myself a promise to leave as soon as I could. To be honest, I don't think the pit ponies enjoyed it much either. They only got out once a year but they never complained.

I was 17 when I remember my father telling me about an important man named Archduke Franz Ferdinand of Austria and his wife who were killed in Sarajevo on 28th June 1914 by some terrorists and this could cause real trouble. I remember him saying that the balloon could go up and I couldn't understand what he meant. It all seemed so far away from me, I had no idea where Sarajevo was – I'm still not too sure!

Anyway, my dad was proved right when he told me that war was declared between England and Germany in August 1914. It didn't seem real but everybody at the pit was talking about it. I was mixed with the men more now because as I was 16 I was allowed to go on the coal face and into the stalls where the men dug the coal, they were called 'hewers' – a funny word I always thought. It would be my future to join them when I was 18.

*Anyway, I can remember seeing posters all over town of an old army officer, a Field Marshall I think, with a big face and a huge bushy moustache; he had a finger pointing at me. The finger followed you however you looked at the poster and it said 'Your country needs **you**!" I was too young when the war started although I always wanted to go; you were supposed to be 19 to start with and then 18 when they wanted more soldiers. My dad told me that I* might have to go but I was also needed in the coal mines as the country needed coal to drive machines to help in the war effort. As I said before, when I was 18 I would be going to work on the coal face and earning a bit more money.

Everybody knew that the war was not going as well as expected. In 1914 the newspapers said it would only last a few weeks. In 1915 after my 18th birthday two things happened. Firstly, young men in our town formed what was called a **'Pals Battalion'** where you could join the army in your own town and you would fight together with pals you knew, mates you had been at school with. The second thing was that, as I was quite tall, people, kept saying to me you ought to be in the trenches. In fact, one woman gave me a white feather which meant that she thought I was a coward and scared to fight. Well, that wasn't true and it really upset me – maybe her husband or brother was at war. I didn't understand at the time but I do now.

So, my dad said it was OK and just after I was 18 I went to join up. I went to the town hall; there were lots of lads lining up. I told the sergeant I was 19 and he just wrote it down and I was signed up as a soldier. I *passed a medical and that was that. I took an oath promising to serve the King and I was in the army.*

"Was this the First World War we learnt about at school," asked Peter.

"It was called that later but, if you think about it, your great great Grandad wouldn't know that there would be another war, so he wouldn't call it the 'First'; they called it the 'Great War'. Anyway, let's carry on."

Peter and his father were totally absorbed in the story. All three wanted to know what happened next and so do I. Jo Bear sat quietly on Peter's knee. I think he already knew the story.

5. Off with my Pals

Grandad cleared his throat, sat back and got on with the story.

Well, within a few days I was saying goodbye to mum and dad and my friends – they were quite proud of me – and off I went on a special train to an army training barracks. By the way, I ought to mention that I took Jo Bear with me in my suitcase, just for good luck. Mind you, I kept him hidden away so as no-one would make fun of me. I needn't have bothered because when we got into the barracks I saw that lots of the lads had brought good luck charms such as pictures, toys, religious things like crosses and rosary beads and even lucky socks or scarves. As it turned out, some lucky charms would work and some would not!

During the training, we had to learn to do some things until we could do them with our eyes closed such as putting the parts of a Lewis machine gun together and cleaning a Lee Enfield Rifle.

We also learnt how to fix bayonets on the end of our rifles, like long carving knives, and then we had to charge at a straw dummy hanging on a frame. You had to scream as you did it – it was frightening but most of the lads quite enjoyed this. It didn't seem so enjoyable later on when we had to run at real people. I don't want to think about that.

We even learnt how to throw grenades, like exploding bombs. Most of us enjoyed the training, it was hard but fun.

We were lucky because we had a proper barrack room to live in during our training; we heard that some recruits had to sleep in tents. There were sergeants and corporals who were in charge; they stamped about and shouted a lot. This upset some lads but not me; colliers shout and swear at lads down the pits worse than any army sergeant! We occasionally saw an officer, they were usually older men. I learnt later that all the young officers were on the front and a lot were killed.

We were supposed to have six months military training but we only had four months before we heard we were to move out to Belgium, wherever that was. By this time we had changed our suitcases for khaki kit bags and we each had own rifle as we were in an infantry regiment. I had a Lee-Enfield bolt action rifle with a wooden end or butt. It looked smart but we quickly learned that unless you cleaned and oiled *your rifle regularly it jammed and wouldn't fire when you really needed it and there would be times when we really needed it.*

We packed up and were marched to the station to board special trains to a port. When we got there, already waiting on the quayside was a huge steam ship. None of my mates had ever seen anything like this and we stood wide-eyed looking at this monster. It seemed to be puffing smoke and chugging even when not moving. 'How does some 'at that big float?' somebody said.

It all seemed very exciting, that was until we saw units of troops filing off the ship. It was not a pleasant sight, they were dirty and miserable looking. Some had bandaged heads, some had only one leg, hoping along with crutches and a lot were being carried on stretchers. There were lines of men with their hands on the shoulder of the man in front and bandages round their eyes, somebody said they'd been gassed.

Before we witnessed this dismal sight we were all excited, laughing and joking but we all went very quiet. It was a shock and it really made us realise that going to war was not going to be fun, not at all! Nobody said anything for a long time. We didn't even look at each other; everybody was lost in their own thoughts. This was going to be serious!

It was too late to change your mind. We learnt later what happened to anyone who wanted to 'change his mind' – they would be shot as cowards and, in fact, a few were.

When the wounded soldiers had got off the ship, the dockers loaded dozens of horses into the hold at the bottom. Then we all piled on the troop ship and set sail to a place named Zeebruge in Belgium. Nearly everybody was sea-sick – it was the first time I had seen the sea let alone been on a ship and that went for most of us. I tried to sleep on my kit bag but it was cold and noisy. Some of the lads were almost in tears but nobody laughed at them. We all sat there engrossed in our own thoughts for most of the crossing but it still wasn't real.

I rumbled about in my kit bag to find a bar of chocolate I had saved for the trip and I saw Jo Bear in the bottom of my bag. I remember telling Jo that this would be the greatest adventure ever, he just looked at me, like he always did - straight into my eyes. Jo wasn't convinced about this and, to be honest, neither was I.

The ship sailed all through the night and we docked around 7 o'clock in the morning. The sergeants had been telling us to try to get some sleep – some hope!

This might have been easier if the lads had not seen the wounded soldiers getting off the ship. Anyway we got off the ship and were packed in railway carriages like cattle wagons and set off clutching our heavy kit bags and rifles. We tried to look brave!

When we got to our destination, I not sure exactly where it was, we were told to get out and form into columns for marching, two abreast. We had been marching for a couple of hours when the sergeants called halt and we all sat on the road edge whilst the cooks made a brew of tea in portable boilers on the back of a cart pulled by two old brown horses. They also produced a box of hard biscuits.

It was while we sat there by the road edge that I heard the first sounds of war, a distant 'boom, boom, boom' of big guns. We had seen a few big guns fired in training but not as many as this, it was almost constant and very frightening. "It's only our lads softening up the Jerries," said a corporal.

I ought to tell you that the kit bag we had to carry weighed up to 30 kilograms. We each had 250 rounds of rifle ammunition, water bottle, haversack, personal stuff such as underclothes and, of course, the rifle and bayonet. Plus one teddy bear.

As we got closer to the noise, we saw more injured soldiers coming the other way. We eventually got to an old farm and we were crowded into a couple of disused barns. The sergeant told us we would get a warm meal and then we should get some sleep as we would be marching to the trenches and the front line tomorrow morning. The warm meal was like weak soup with knobs of crusty, stale bread – but we were hungry.

So far so good, we didn't quite know what to expect next. This was not like our training at all! I thought everybody would be chattering like they did during the training but they didn't. It was quiet, too quiet.

I remember having the same feeling when I was waiting to get into the cage to go down the pit for the first time. You know, trying to look brave but not feeling brave.

6. Off to the Front

In the morning I looked out of the barn door and noticed that all the trees were broken like weird twisted sticks pointing out of the ground, all the hedges were flattened and, really oddly, we were in the middle of the countryside but there was no bird song – none at all.

We had a breakfast of sweet porridge and then we all lined up for a talk from one of the officers. He was a smart young man, a captain but not much older than me, he talked with a posh voice, smiled and seemed very confident. I can't remember all he said but it went something like this . . .

"You lads are lucky to be here at this important time, in years to come your friends will regret not being here. You are going to see some sights you will not enjoy but we are gaining a real advantage and we shall win in the end. Remember, you fight for your King and for your Country and, remember most of all, to do exactly what your officers, sergeants and corporals say without question. That is the only way we are going to win this war. Good luck, God bless the King and God bless all of you."

For some reason we all stood up and cheered for him, I don't know why but we just did. We then formed up in three ranks and marched to the front line. The closer we got the louder the sound of guns became much louder. So loud that you couldn't really tell which direction they were coming from. The 'boom, boom, boom' of the big artillery pieces was supported by rifle fire and the rattle of machine guns.

The ground was soaking wet, with sludge, puddles and deep cart tracks everywhere. Every tree was smashed and twisted, I couldn't see one complete tree still standing. There was twisted barbed wire everywhere and the stench was really sickening. We passed more wounded men; we saw some men who looked as though they were dead and some dead horses. I felt really sorry for the horses, they couldn't defend themselves and they certainly didn't volunteer. It reminded me of my friends, the pit ponies; I wondered of any of them were here.

I had never seen anyone dead before; I soon got used to that! We walked past a crowd of men sitting on the wet ground surrounded by some soldiers pointing their guns at them. "Jerry prisoners," shouted the sergeant, "look at their bloody evil faces."

Well, I looked at them as I marched past but to be honest again, they didn't look evil they looked like frightened young men - just like we were, wondering what brought them there.

"Who are 'Jerries' Grandad?"

"Well, Peter, it was a sort of nickname the British soldiers used at that time. In fact they were German soldiers. I think the Germans called our troops 'Tommies'. Do you want me to carry on?" Peter and his father nodded enthusiastically. Peter looked at his father and noticed that his eyes were wide open – he was amazed.

Grandad cleared his throat yet again, adjusted his spectacles and set off. You could tell he was deeply involved in the story.

As we approached the front line we were told to keep our heads down and file into the back of a zig-zig line of trenches. These trenches were a system of deep ditches, just deep enough so that you could walk without your head sticking out the top, about six feet (almost 2 metres). We quickly found out that sticking your head up was not a good idea, not very clever at all. The trenches, wide enough for two men to pass carrying their kit bags, were dirty, smelly and wet; some had wooden boards at the bottom to walk on and some didn't. We even saw some big rats scuttling along and totally ignoring us, as if they were there first.

We had seen mock-up trenches at the training camp but they were not as wet and dirty and they didn't smell quite the same!

At the back of the trenches there were sleeping quarters like a small cave or room dug into the earth and supported by wooden beams or props, a little bit like the stalls down our coal mine. We relieved another group and those that could walk shuffled out in single file. Some had to be helped out and some were on stretchers. They didn't say much. One guy looked at me with his muddy face and said, "Good luck mate, you'll need it." I just smiled; I didn't know what to say. It was all new at this stage.

The sergeant passed along the line. He tried to whisper but he had a naturally loud voice and even his whisper was loud and booming. That's maybe why he was a sergeant I thought.

"Unpack your kit, get in your bivouac, and get some food and sleep. We're over the top on the second phase tomorrow. Keep your heads down, you don't want to give them jerry snipers any target practice."

I found a dirty damp corner and settled down. When I emptied my kit bag I placed Jo Bear on my pillow. Well not really a pillow just a bullet pouch and a spare woollen vest. When it got dark the guns stopped and everything seemed to go quiet. It was eerie, as if everyone on both sides were resting. I think I got some sleep as I was tired out. I was woken up by the thunderous sound of what seemed like hundreds of guns firing from behind us and the shells whistling over our heads. Our corporal told us it was our artillery 'softening up the enemy' before the attack. I think he said this before - several times.

When we were all in our battle kit we crouched down in the thick sticky, smelly mud. An old soldier walked along the line with a big stone jar and shouting, "Hold out your cans!" He poured in a measure of a thick, dark liquid which turned out to be rum or whisky or something like that. I drank it and it made my head spin. I was not used to drinking; I'd only had some beer when my dad was not looking. They used to give us this stuff almost every day, probably to warm us up.

The guns stopped as suddenly as they had started and for a short time everything went quiet – no noise from either side. Then I heard a series of high-pitched whistles. The squad of soldiers next along the trench to us scrabbled up the wooden ladders and over the top of the trench; they we all shouting and screaming. The young officers always went over first holding out their pistols at arm's length and then the lads with their rifles. The sergeants pushed them all up the ladder and then went at the back. As soon as they got over the top I heard the sound of machine fire and I saw several of the squad just along from us fly back into the trench covered in blood. I realised they had been shot. The noise was tremendous!

It was all happening around us and I didn't know where to look. It was hard to take it all in – it was our first real experience of war. It became routine and we learnt to accept death as normal. Looking back I can hardly relieve this but it was true.

Anyway, our turn came next and it didn't take long. I was third up the ladder. The first guy was shot in front of me. I managed to run forward for a few minutes before dropping down into a bomb crater – knee deep in water. I scrambled to the edge and fired at the machine gun flashes, I don't know if I hit anyone. Someone shouted 'pull back' so I scrambled back over the mud, bits of barbed wire, the puddles and also bodies of some of the soldiers I had been crouched down with a few minutes before. It all happened so quickly. Machine gun bullets were flying over our heads right up to the point I stumbled back into the trench, totally exhausted. The sergeant shouted, "Well done lads, we gave them hell."

I didn't really feel like we had but nevertheless, we congratulated each other – our first real action!

When the stretcher bearers went out at dusk to retrieve the dead and injured, I wondered who had won what! I didn't realise how time had flown, we had been over the top, in what they call 'no man's land' for almost two hours. A man came along with a wooden box full of bullets and we re-stocked our ammunition pouches. Then the sergeant worked his way down the trench with a big ledger and took a roll-call and, as he ticked off the names, there were too many mates who didn't answer his call.

We did this twice during that day and each time more mates were injured and some killed. As I laid down in the dark I tried to tell Jo Bear what a nightmare it had been. I had to tell somebody. I don't think he understood, I couldn't really understand it myself but he must have heard the noise.

This same tactics went on most days for over a long, long week. It was terrible but I don't want to repeat it all again in my story, but take my word for it. But it was to get even worse, month after once and year after year.

Sometimes we made ground and sometimes we were pushed back by the enemy. Sometimes we even did nothing at all for over a week or two, just sat there deep in our own thoughts. I thought that working down the coal mine was not such a bad job after all.

7. A Backward Step

"*Do you want me to make a cup of tea,*" asked Grandad breaking off from the story.

"*No, Grandad, we're just getting to the best bit, keep going.*"

"*Is this all true?*" Peter's dad was not so sure.

"*Yes, I'm certain it is, why would he write it all down like this, it's not a thing you make up, is it?*" Grandad was totally convinced and why shouldn't he be. He turned back to the old notebook.

It became clear that we were not making any progress and were definitely losing more men, injured or even killed. The sergeant kept saying it would be OK, "It's OK lads," he would say to us, "they've promised reinforcements tomorrow." Or, "you're doing a great job, it'll all be over soon."

I remembered what my dad said to me down the pit, when a wooden pit prop split, "Don't leave it until tomorrow lad, because tomorrow never comes." I now know what he meant.

Early one bright morning we were sitting in the trench when an officer scrambled into our trench over the mud from the back of our lines and dropped down at the side of us. He was carrying a wooden pole with a white circle on the top. It was the same captain who had been talking to us a month's ago, or was it years – they all merged into one. "Things will be OK, lads, I've just been to an officers' meeting and reinforcements are on their way." Where have I heard this before, I thought to myself?

"I've got to go into 'no man's land' and set a target marker for the artillery. What's your name lad?"

"Private Albert Clarkson sir," I stood up to say it, you had to do that when you spoke to an officer.

He passed me a single sheet of paper from his tunic top pocket, "Look Clarkson, this is a note listing the reinforcements and the dates of their planned arrival; I got it from the General at our staff meeting this morning. If anything should happen to me out there I don't want the Germans to get hold of this. Keep it for me and I'll have it when I get back and before you and your mates go over the top." He then smiled at me, turned round and shinned up the ladder at the front of the trench, disappearing into the breaking dawn light and the dangerous 'no man's land' with his little wooden pole.

Wow, I thought to myself, what a really brave guy. I'm going ahead of my story, but I need to write down that I never ever saw that brave young officer again. I don't know what happened to him but I suspect it wasn't good!

About an hour later our artillery started firing over our heads. I knew we would be in action very soon. I still had the note in my hand. It suddenly occurred to me that if anything happened to me, the note could still fall into enemy hands. The officer didn't come back and I decided to leave the note in the trench, but where? I went into the dug-out looking for a hiding place when I saw Jo Bear sitting in the corner. I folded the note and placed it, out of sight, in the little pocket that Jo had on his tummy. "Guard that with your life, I'll be back as soon as I can," I promised Jo. This was a promise that, unfortunately, I would not be able to keep.

It wasn't long before we heard the whistles and went up the wooden ladders and over the top. Almost immediately we found the enemy machine gun fire to be closer to our trench and much heavier than we expected. Soldiers were dropping everywhere. "Pull back," screamed an officer, "Pull back!" I followed him back into our trench. "The Bosch must have moved up overnight, we're got to withdraw."

The few of us who were left followed the officer out of the trench and we crawled back over the muddy ground. When it was safe we ran and finally walked or crawled back towards where we came from in the first place, weeks ago. We saw others retreating across the mud. I thought to myself, what a waste, but I didn't say anything. We were all exhausted.

Suddenly I realised that I had left all my kit behind and, more importantly, Jo bear was still sitting on my make-shift pillow. I was responsible for Jo and now I had lost him in this terrible place. In one way I felt sadder about Jo that my mates – don't get me wrong, I knew he was only a teddy bear, but I was responsible for Jo, just me. Then I remembered that Jo had the note from the captain about reinforcements in his little pocket. Would the Germans find it? Would Jo keep the secret?

A few dozen of us ended up in some old trenches about a mile or so further back. I didn't know what was going to happen but I thought of Jo sitting all alone and maybe getting blown to pieces as the Germans advanced. I thought he must be really scared because I had seen rats in the trenches almost as big as Jo Bear himself. I decided not to say anything about the note to anyone and I certainly wasn't going to say anything about Jo Bear.

After a few days of quiet, we learnt that the Germans had taken over our trenches and were expected to attack our lines from that position when we least expected it.

Everybody was very depressed at losing so many mates and also so much ground, we felt we were to blame but we had only done what we were told. Things settled down for a week or so then we were told we had reinforcements and were going to push forward again. We thought it was just the same thing all over again.

More clean, bright, young British soldiers filled the system of trenches and on the next day our artillery started firing as soon as it was dawn. A few minutes afterwards the guns stopped and we went over the top. There seemed to be thousands of us as far as you could see on both sides. There was some machine fire but not as much and we made good progress. After scrambling through the bullets, mud, barbed wire and shell craters we reached the trench system we left before the retreat. The Germans seemed to be falling back now. We could see them scrambling back and many were falling injured or dead. A sergeant told us to drop into a trench and take a rest. I slide down the mud and sat on the duck boards at the bottom of the trench. You no longer seemed to bother about the water or the smell. It's amazing what you can get used to if you have to.

As we sat in the mud getting our breath and waiting for further orders, I looked round at the sides of the trench and noticed some of the same drawings on the boards that my mates had made last time we were here. I realised we were in the very same trench! Suddenly a thought flashed into my head, Jo Bear! I found the same dug-out that we lived in and crawled through the door, well not a door but an opening. I found the corner I slept in and I found the old vest I used as a pillow – but no Jo. I searched all around the dug-out, no Jo. What did I expect; this is a war not a play room!

As I went to the door, although, as I said, there was no actual door it was just a hole, I had to stoop as the dug-out was not high enough to stand up in. For some reason I looked up and I saw a little cubby hole that had been carved out of the earth by the side of the opening. Would you believe it, sitting in the little alcove was nobody else but Jo Bear. He was sitting on a piece of stone and looking straight into my eyes. I took him down just to check it was indeed Jo. Yes, it was, same fur, same eyes, same Jo. A little dirtier but it was the same bear. I dipped my fingers into his pocket and found that the little note was still there, no-

one had taken it. It was probably the last place they would look. When I asked Jo to guard it with his life I wasn't serious, really – but he had, he had and I was proud of him!

I wondered who had taken the time to look after him. You had gently placed him in the cubby hole - it must have been one of the German soldiers! I couldn't believe it. Jo had actually been in the trenches with the enemy and carrying a secret document! I put the little note back in Jo's pocket. I packed him carefully into my kit bag. I decided not to leave him alone again – whatever happens. But, this was another promise I would be unable to keep.

8. Getting our own back!

The next day the officers decided that we must attack again to push the Germans back even further to reinforce our gains. So we were over the top and attacking once more, this time Jo was safe in my kit bag and we all took everything with us – not that we had a great deal of stuff.

It is all very blurred but I remember rushing across 'no man's land' and firing at some Germans. I remember cutting through some barbed wire and running towards the German lines. I ducked as an artillery shell landed in the ground in-between where I was crouching with my mates, we were all splattered with dirt and mud. I'm not really sure whether it was a German shell or one of our own – it was all a confused mess to us.

Another shell landed in the same hole but didn't immediately explode as they normally did. I could see the others just looking at it in total terror, waiting for the bang. I picked up a big piece of corrugated metal sheeting that was at the bottom of the hole and slammed it over the shell, holding it down with my body weight. Then everything went black, I can't remember anything else after that other than a huge black cloud dropping very slowly from the sky – a weird feeling.

Later on, I don't know how long, I woke up briefly to find myself lying on a stretcher with a medic leaning over me with a syringe in his hand. "One with your name on it, mate," he said before pushing the syringe needle into my arm. The same black cloud dropped again but faster this time. Was this what dying was like?

"What does that mean Grandad, one with your name on it?" asked Peter, who was listening very carefully and taking in every word.

"The soldiers used to say that if a German bullet or shell had your name on it there was nothing you could do. It was a way of making sense of the fact that some were shot and some never got a scratch."

I wasn't dead because the next time I woke up I was in a hospital bed back in England. I had bandages on my legs, across my chest and around my head. "Hello," said a friendly looking nurse, "we didn't expect you to come back to us, you were pretty badly cut up. You had a close shave!"

"What happened?"

"Well, as far as I know you were very close to a shell when it exploded. In a way it seems you are lucky to be alive."

I lay in bed for several weeks thinking about my mates, many who would not be coming home, and if I would ever get back to the pit again. I also thought about Jo Bear. He was in my kit bag and he must have been blown to pieces. It was a sad end for a very brave bear who had been protecting one of our military secrets. I had some bad dreams in that hospital and, at one stage, thought I would be better off dead.

However, I did get a little better. One day, when I was sitting in my wheelchair outside the hospital, I was told I had to go to see an officer. I was pushed to the back garden of the hospital by an orderly where I saw several men lined up and some officers standing by a table. I recognised one of the officers to be the very same old man who I saw on the poster many years ago, you remember, the one with the big bushy moustache – the one who was pointing his finger at me!

He made a short speech about winning the war and about brave young men. Then, followed by a young officer carrying a wooden tray of medals, he went along the line of injured men lined up on the grass.

When it came to my turn, the officer told those around me that I had received my injuries when I dived on a live shell just before it exploded. He said I had saved the lives of several men and because of my bravery I was to be awarded the Military Medal. He pinned a silver medal with a blue, red and white ribbon on my pyjama jacket. He shook my hand and everybody applauded. I didn't know what to say, I could only remember little bits of this. Nobody told me I was to get a bravery medal. Then I had another thought, I may have been brave but I hadn't been able to save Jo Bear.

I just said thank you sir, I'm sorry I can't get up. He smiled and went to the next soldier – that was that.

That was it, the whole story, well not quite the whole story I left out a lot of the detail, stuff I don't really want to remember. I jumped several years in my story as they were all the same. I eventually got better and apart from some metal stuck in my head for ever, I went back home to get fully fit. I couldn't go underground anymore so I was looking for a new job.

I never told anyone about the medal or about Jo and the secret note. I had four medals, I never wore them and I never showed them to anyone.

Then Stan came to see me, as I explained at the beginning. The story is finished and on the last page I wrote . . .

I was awarded the Military Medal for bravery but I was never as brave as this little brown bear. I award the medal to Joseph Bear MM.

"What's going on here, you all look as though you've seen a ghost," grandma walked in dropping her heavy shopping on the table.

"Maybe we have, mum, maybe we have" said Peter's dad.

"Are you crying?" asked grandma looking at her son.

"No, I've just got a cold." Peter looked at his dad; he did have tears rolling down his face.

"I think I had better put the kettle on," and off she went.

We all know that Jo Bear has lived a very long life and now he lives with Peter. Now he knows the real story, I am sure that Peter will look after Jo Bear for ever. Unless, of course, he passes him on to his son!

The Bravest Bear I know

It all goes to show that even someone who looks dirty and scruffy can be a hero and can be brave, like Jo Bear. You never know and you must never jump to a conclusion, even about a teddy bear!

The end.

Made in the USA
Charleston, SC
18 November 2014